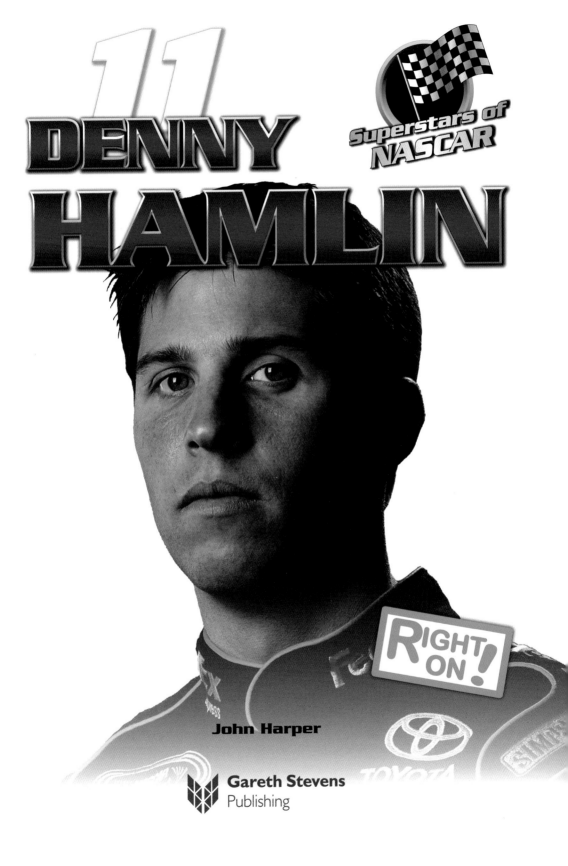

11 DENNY HAMLIN

Superstars of NASCAR

RIGHT ON!

John Harper

Gareth Stevens
Publishing

Please visit our Web site, www.garethstevens.com. For a free color catalog of all our high-quality books, call toll free 1-800-542-2595 or fax 1-877-542-2596.

Library of Congress Cataloging-in-Publication Data

Harper, John, 1976-
Denny Hamlin / John Harper.
    p. cm. —(Superstars of NASCAR)
Includes index.
ISBN 978-1-4339-3951-8 (pbk.)
ISBN 978-1-4339-3952-5 (6-pack)
ISBN 978-1-4339-3950-1 (library binding)
1. Hamlin, Denny, 1980—Juvenile literature. 2. Stock car drivers—United States—Biography—Juvenile literature. 3. Automobile racing drivers—United States—Biography—Juvenile literature. I. Title.
 GV1032.H24H37 2010
 796.72092—dc22
 [B]
                              2010008167

First Edition

Published in 2011 by
Gareth Stevens Publishing
111 East 14th Street, Suite 349
New York, NY 10003

Designer: Michael J. Flynn
Editor: Mary Ann Hoffman

Photo credits: Cover (Denny Hamlin), pp. 1, 9, 19 Rusty Jarrett/Getty Images; cover, pp. 4, 6, 8, 12, 14, 16, 18, 20, 24, 26, 28 (background for all) Shutterstock.com; pp. 5, 29 Chris Graythen/Getty Images; p. 7 Streeter Lecka/Getty Images; pp. 10–11, 25 Geoff Burke/Getty Images; p. 13 Todd Warshaw/Getty Images; p. 15 John Harrelson/ Getty Images; p. 17 Doug Benc/Getty Images; p. 21 Chris Trotman/Getty Images; pp. 22–23 Robert Laberge/Getty Images; p. 27 Jason Smith/Getty Images.

Printed in the United States of America

CPSIA compliance information: Batch #CS10GS: For further information contact Gareth Stevens, New York, New York at 1-800-542-2595.

Contents

A Race Car Driver

Denny Hamlin is a driver in the
NASCAR Sprint Cup Series.
He was born in Virginia on
November 18, 1980.

Go-Karts

Denny began racing at the age of 7. He raced go-karts. Go-karts are very small, open-body cars.

7

Denny was racing mini stock cars by the time he was 16. He was the youngest driver to win the NASCAR Mini Stock track championship.

Denny Hamlin

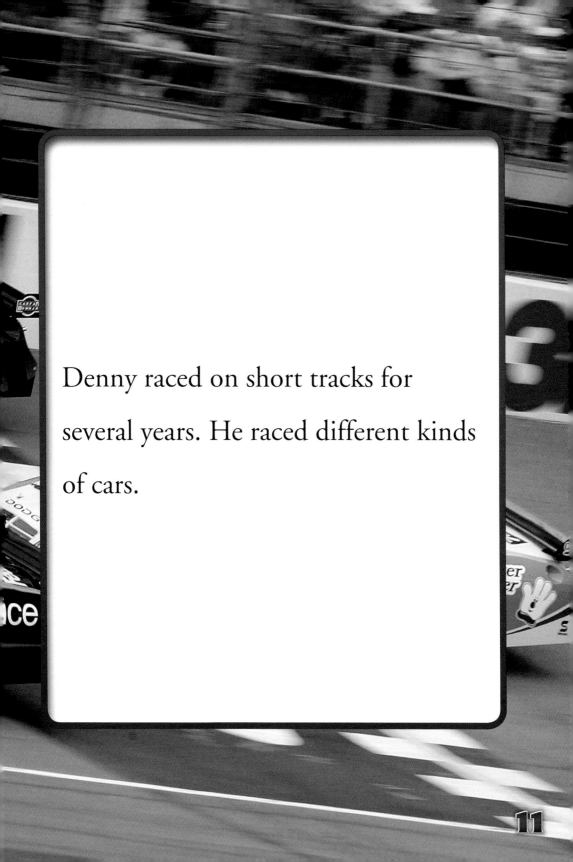

Denny raced on short tracks for several years. He raced different kinds of cars.

A NASCAR Team

NASCAR team owner Joe Gibbs noticed Denny's driving skills. In 2004, Denny became a driver for Joe Gibbs Racing.

Joe Gibbs

13

Trucks and Cars

Denny raced in the NASCAR truck series. He drove in the Nationwide Series, too. This series is one level below the Sprint Cup Series.

At the age of 24, Denny raced in the Nationwide Series for the whole season. He finished fifth in points.

17

Denny began racing in the Sprint Cup Series in 2006. He won a big race at Daytona Speedway and another at Pocono Raceway.

19

A Great Success

Denny was named Rookie of the Year in 2006. He had one of the most successful first seasons ever in the Sprint Cup Series.

DENNY HAMLIN - 2006

21

Denny Hamlin

In the 2007 and 2008 seasons, Denny won two Sprint Cup races. He had 24 top-5 finishes and 36 top-10 finishes.

In 2008, Denny also raced in the
Nationwide Series. He won four out
of 19 races.

A Winning Season

In 2009, Denny had his best Sprint Cup season since his first year. He led the final race of the season for 70 laps!

Denny has accomplished a lot during his years with Joe Gibbs Racing. He continues to want to be the best!

Timeline

1980 Denny is born in Virginia.

1997 Denny wins NASCAR Mini Stock track championship.

2004 Denny joins Joe Gibbs Racing.

2006 Denny wins a big race at Daytona Speedway.

2006 Denny is named Rookie of the Year.

2009 Denny wins four races and finishes fifth in points.

For More Information

Books:

Sawyer, Sarah. *Denny Hamlin: NASCAR Driver*. New York, NY: Rosen Central, 2009.

Stewart, Mark, and Mike Kennedy. *NASCAR Safety on the Track*. Minneapolis, MN: Lerner Publications Co., 2008.

Web Sites:

Denny Hamlin—Biography
www.dennyhamlin.com/page.php?_=bio

Denny Hamlin #11
sports.espn.go.com/rpm/driver?driverid=747

Glossary

championship: a series of races to decide a winner

mini stock car: a less-powerful racing car that looks like a regular car

rookie: a person in their first year of a sport

Sprint Cup Series: the top racing series of NASCAR

Index